To Admiral Pat DeQuattro, my lifelong friend who exemplifies
to me what it means be American. —RD

To my stepfather, Leonard, a natural-born American, who taught me about service to America;
to my father, Chaim, a naturalized American, who helped me understand…and
to my children, who have yet to learn what it means to be American. —EY

To my Lolo Bano, Aria, and to all the dreamers, the doers,
and the protectors of our freedom. —NM

Text © 2019 by March 4th, Inc.
Text by Rana DiOrio and Elad Yoran
Illustrations © 2019 by Nina Mata
Cover and internal design © 2019 by Allison Sundstrom/Sourcebooks, Inc.
Sourcebooks and the colophon are registered trademarks of Sourcebooks, Inc.
All art was digitally created using Adobe Photoshop CC.
Published by Little Pickle Press, an imprint of Sourcebooks Jabberwocky.
P.O. Box 4410, Naperville, Illinois 60567-4410
(630) 961-3900
Fax: (630) 961-2168
sourcebooks.com
Library of Congress Cataloging-in-Publication Data is on file with the publisher.
Source of Production: Hung Hing Off-Set Printing Co., Ltd.,
Shenzhen, Guangdong Province, China
Date of Production: January 2019
Run Number: 5013907
Printed and bound in China
HH 10 9 8 7 6 5 4 3 2 1

What Does It Mean to Be American?

by **Rana DiOrio & Elad Yoran**
Pictures by **Nina Mata**

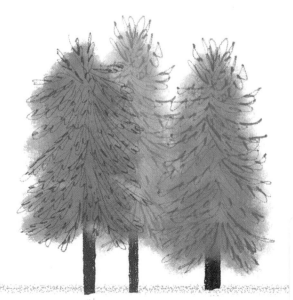

Little
Pickle
Press

What does it mean to be American?

Does it mean liking apple pie and fireworks?

No.

Does it mean living in the United States?

Not exactly.

Does it mean loving fast food?

No.

Being American means…

believing that all people are equal,

and should have the
opportunity to be happy.

...following our dreams,

and working hard
to achieve them.

…having the freedom to choose
whom we love, what we believe, what we do, and where we live,

and to change our minds
if we want.

...knowing all Americans

follow the same rules.

...honoring those

who protect and serve us.

…cherishing our abundant natural resources,

and enjoying time spent outdoors.

...being grateful all year for our many blessings,

and leading by example to take action
when people need help.

…welcoming people from other countries and helping them learn what it means to be American.

...appreciating that
our differences make us kinder,

smarter,

healthier, and stronger.

…using our imagination and creativity to invent new things, and our curiosity and courage to explore new frontiers.

...being proud of all we have accomplished,
and humble about all we still need to learn.

Being American means…

having the right to become your best self,
and the obligation to help others do so too.

So fill your heart with love for who we are,
and your mind with ideas of how you,
your family, and your friends can make
the greatest nation in the world…

even better.

A Note to Caring Adults from the Authors

There are children's books that discuss America and Americana, however there are few that introduce this important topic to younger children. We believe that it is never too early for a child to understand the essence of what it means to be American, which is why we wrote this book. Our intention is to give caring adults the opportunity to start meaningful conversations about the many aspects of what it means to be American. The following information is meant to catalyze those discussions by providing examples of the inspiration for our book as well as posing thoughtful questions for you to share. We welcome your feedback regarding what this book has meant to you and what materials you would like to support your quest to discover what it means to be American. Our objective is to strengthen our nation by fostering pride, raising awareness, and building community. You may reach us at hello@beamerican.io.

Thank you for your commitment to upholding the ideals that make America so special.

God bless America,

Rana & Elad

Being American means believing that all people are equal, and should have the opportunity to be happy.

The ideal of equality is the foundational American value as first articulated in the Declaration of Independence. Here is an excerpt:

In Congress, July 4, 1776.

The unanimous Declaration of the thirteen united States of America, When in the Course of human events, it becomes necessary for one people to dissolve the political bands which have connected them with another, and to assume among the powers of the earth, the separate and equal station to which the Laws of Nature and of Nature's God entitle them, a decent respect to the opinions of mankind requires that they should declare the causes which impel them to the separation.

We hold these truths to be self-evident, that all men are created equal, that they are endowed by their Creator with certain unalienable Rights, that among these are Life, Liberty and the pursuit of Happiness.—That to secure these rights, Governments are instituted among Men, deriving their just powers from the consent of the governed, —That whenever any Form of Government becomes destructive of these ends, it is the Right of the People to alter or to abolish it, and to institute new Government, laying its foundation on such principles and organizing its powers in such form, as to them shall seem most likely to effect their Safety and Happiness.

★ What does it look like for people to be treated equally? What are some examples of not being treated equally? How does equality give people the *opportunity* to be happy?

• • • ━━━━━━━━━━━━━━━━━━━━━━━━━━━━━━━━━━━━━ • • •

Being American means following our dreams, and working hard to achieve them.

Throughout history, Americans have come from humble beginnings to lead extraordinary lives. The following are just a few examples:

- **Abraham Lincoln**, who was born in a one-room log cabin, became the sixteenth president of the United States.
- **Ella Fitzgerald**, who prevailed over much adversity including the loss of her mother at age fifteen, became the First Lady of Song.
- **Helen Keller**, who overcame obstacles from being deaf and blind, became an accomplished activist and author.
- **Jackie Robinson**, who came from a poor family during segregation, became the first African American to play Major League Baseball.
- **Sandra Day O'Connor**, who grew up on a ranch without electricity, became the first woman to serve on the Supreme Court.

- **Simone Biles**, who was once a foster child, became one of the most decorated American gymnasts.
- **Susan B. Anthony**, who endured social ridicule and hardship, became a passionate advocate for women's rights and the women's suffrage movement.
- **Walt Disney**, who followed his dreams despite several financial setbacks, became a pioneer in the American animated film and amusement park industries.

★ Can you think of other Americans who worked hard to achieve great things? What is one of your dreams, and how do you plan to work hard to achieve it?

Being American means having the freedom to choose whom we love, what we believe, what we do, and where we live, and to change our minds if we want.

The U.S. Constitution was written as the framework of our country's government. But as a country develops, sometimes the framework needs adjustments. The Bill of Rights makes up the first ten amendments to the U.S. Constitution, and it laid out the American ideals of freedoms, liberties, and rights. The following are excerpts from the Bill of Rights:

Amendment I

Congress shall make no law respecting an establishment of religion, or prohibiting the free exercise thereof; or abridging the freedom of speech, or of the press; or the right of the people peaceably to assemble, and to petition the Government for a redress of grievances.

Amendment II

A well regulated Militia, being necessary to the security of a free State, the right of the people to keep and bear Arms, shall not be infringed.

★ Who are some people you love? How do you know you love them? What do you believe about religion? How is that similar to or different from your friends?

Being American means knowing all Americans follow the same rules.

Each of the states that make up the United States has its own set of laws. And individual counties and cities within each state have their own ordinances. But the country as a whole follows the federal laws outlined by the U.S. Constitution. The following is the preamble, or introduction, to the Constitution:

We the People of the United States, in Order to form a more perfect Union, establish Justice, insure domestic Tranquility, provide for the common defence, promote the general Welfare, and secure the Blessings of Liberty to ourselves and our Posterity, do ordain and establish this Constitution for the United States of America.

★ What are some of the rules you are expected to follow at home? At school? In your community? Why do you think it's important that everyone follows the same rules?

Being American means honoring those who protect and serve us.

Several national holidays exist to honor those in our country's armed forces. The reverence we have for our military was eloquently captured in President Abraham Lincoln's Gettysburg Address on November 19, 1863:

Four score and seven years ago our fathers brought forth, on this continent, a new nation, conceived in Liberty, and dedicated to the proposition that all men are created equal. Now we are engaged in a great civil war, testing whether that nation, or any nation so conceived and so dedicated, can long endure. We are met on a great battle-field of that war. We have come to dedicate a portion of that field, as a final resting-place for those who here gave their lives that that nation might live. It is altogether fitting and proper that we should do this. But, in a larger sense, we cannot dedicate—we cannot consecrate—we cannot hallow—this ground. The brave men, living and dead, who struggled here, have consecrated it, far above our poor power to add or detract. The world will little note, nor long remember what we say here, but it can never forget what they did here. It is for us the living, rather, to be dedicated here to the unfinished work which they who fought here have thus far so nobly advanced. It is rather for us to be here dedicated to the great task remaining before us—that from these honored dead we take increased devotion to that cause for which they here gave the last full measure of devotion—that we here highly resolve that these dead shall not have died in vain—that this nation, under God, shall have a new birth of freedom—and that government of the people, by the people, for the people, shall not perish from the earth.

★ Besides the military, what other jobs exist to protect and serve you and your community? In what ways can you honor their service? Who are people in your community whose job it is to serve and protect?

Being American means cherishing our abundant natural resources, and enjoying time spent outdoors.

Our country has one of the most diverse landscapes in the world. We have fertile land for farming. We also have beautiful scenery to visit—from deserts to mountains to sandy beaches and lakes. Love and appreciation for the abundance America offers its citizens and visitors has been vividly captured by many songs, such as "America the Beautiful." The following is an excerpt:

O beautiful for spacious skies,
For amber waves of grain,
For purple mountain majesties
Above the fruited plain!
America! America!
God shed His grace on thee,
And crown thy good with brotherhood
From sea to shining sea!

★ Take a look outside. What does the landscape look like around you? Have you visited other parts of America that look different from where you live?

Being American means being grateful all year for our many blessings.

President Abraham Lincoln declared Thanksgiving a national holiday in 1863. Every year since then, families gather to celebrate all the things they are thankful for, typically while sharing a meal. Celebrating in this grand way once a year is particularly powerful, but being grateful all year is important too.

★ What are some things you are grateful for? How do you show your gratitude?

Being American means leading by example to take action when people need help.

Americans are known to help others in times of need. One example of this is Clara Barton, who was a nurse during the American Civil War and was later inspired to found the American Red Cross.

★ What are some ways that you help others? Describe a time when someone helped you.

• • • ━━━━━━━━━━━━━━━━━━━━━━━━━━━━━━ • • •

Being American means welcoming people from other countries and helping them learn what it means to be American…and appreciating that our differences make us kinder, smarter, healthier, and stronger.

America is a nation made up of many different kinds of people. In the late 1800s to mid-1900s, more than twelve million immigrants entered the United States through Ellis Island, the federal immigration processing station in New York Harbor. Nowadays, an average of about one million immigrants enter the U.S. annually. And approximately seven hundred thousand people become naturalized citizens each year. The ideal that America welcomes all people shines through Emma Lazarus's poem, "The New Colossus," which appears on a plaque on the Statue of Liberty:

> Not like the brazen giant of Greek fame,
> With conquering limbs astride from land to land;
> Here at our sea-washed, sunset gates shall stand
> A mighty woman with a torch, whose flame
> Is the imprisoned lightning, and her name
> Mother of Exiles. From her beacon-hand
> Glows world-wide welcome; her mild eyes command
> The air-bridged harbor that twin cities frame.
> "Keep, ancient lands, your storied pomp!" cries she
> With silent lips. "Give me your tired, your poor,
> Your huddled masses yearning to breathe free,
> The wretched refuse of your teeming shore.
> Send these, the homeless, tempest-tost to me,
> I lift my lamp beside the golden door!"

★ America is a country with many immigrants. Among your family and friends, how many different countries of origin can you identify before America?

Being American means using our imagination and creativity to invent new things and our curiosity and courage to explore new frontiers…and being proud of all we have accomplished and humble about all we still need to learn.

Many Americans have been pioneers of their respective industries—whether they're manufacturers, scientists, artists, engineers, writers, musicians, civil servants, doctors, or creative thinkers. For example, automobiles did not exist before people invented them, and ever since then, people from all over the world have worked to improve upon them time after time. This is an example of how imagination and creativity can lead to invention, and yet we are never done learning how things could be better. Here are a few examples of Americans who were creative and innovative in different ways:

- **Grace Hopper**, a mathematician and U.S. Navy rear admiral, was an early pioneer in computer programming languages and was posthumously awarded the Presidential Medal of Freedom.
- **Leonard Bernstein**, a composer, conductor, and pianist, was one of the first conductors born and educated in the United States to achieve international fame.
- **Samuel Langhorne Clemens (a.k.a. Mark Twain)**, a writer, humorist, entrepreneur, publisher, and lecturer, has been called "the father of American literature."

- **Steve Jobs**, an entrepreneur, businessman, inventor, and industrial designer, revolutionized the way people forge relationships with their personal technology.
- **Temple Grandin**, a professor of animal science and animal behavior expert, is one of the first people to speak openly about her experiences with having autism. She is a respected autism advocate and was recognized by *Time* magazine as one of the most influential people in the world in 2010.

★ Find three physical things around you and discover who invented or created each one. Then learn about what improvements were made to the first version to get to the one you see now. For example, if you see a cell phone nearby, who invented it? What did the first cell phone look like? How has the technology changed? How would you design an even better cell phone?

• • • ━━ • • •

Being American means having the right to become your best self and the obligation to help others do so too.

To continue growing and improving our nation, it is important for us all to work together and help each other whenever we can. This is how YOU can become the best example of what it means to be American!

Rana DiOrio is a third-generation Italian American who is deeply proud of her Italian heritage and family. As a child, she was fascinated by the stories of how her ancestors came to live in the United States, the sacrifices they made to be American, and the hardships they overcame to remain American. Her parents were educators who imbued in her a love of learning and a commitment to serving others. Her relatives have served in the armed forces during World War I, World War II, the Korean War, and the Vietnam War.

Becoming a mother inspired Rana to find a way to align her career and values. Her solution was to become an entrepreneur, founding March 4, Inc. (formerly Little Pickle Press) in 2009 as a social mission company dedicated to creating media and products that foster kindness in children, including her own. Her personal pursuits include fitness training; practicing yoga; traveling; reading nonfiction and children's books; dreaming big dreams and helping others realize theirs; and, of course, being global, green, present, safe, kind, entrepreneurial, and American. She lives in San Francisco, California, with her three children. Follow Rana DiOrio on Twitter @ranadiorio.

Elad Yoran is the first American-born child of immigrant parents. When he was growing up, his family moved several times and he lived in several places including New York, California, Ohio, and Israel before settling in the NYC suburbs. When he graduated from high school, Elad decided to serve in the U.S. Army as a way of giving back for all that this country has done for his family. He graduated from the United States Military Academy at West Point and served as a paratrooper and officer in the U.S. Army, leading a platoon in Mogadishu, Somalia, as part of Operation Restore Hope. He is married and together with his wife has four children whom they are raising to be both proud of their heritage and patriotic Americans.

Elad also spends time as Executive Chairman of KoolSpan and CEO of Security Growth Partners. He is a twenty-plus-year cybersecurity veteran, among other things having created and led many foundational cyber start-up companies, for which he was honored as "Entrepreneur of the Year" by Ernst & Young. He serves on several government and industry boards including the Army Cyber Institute, the Cloud Security Alliance, and previously, the FBI IT Advisory Council. Elad is the author of many cyber articles and papers. This is his first children's book. The Yorans live in New York City.

Nina Mata grew up as a typical latchkey kid from Queens, New York. Her family emigrated from the Philippines when she was six years old. Because her parents worked and went to night school, Nina spent a lot (like a whole lot) of time drawing. Her after-school activities usually involved watching Bob Ross and *Reading Rainbow*, and finding adventure in books.

She studied commercial arts at the High School of Art & Design and went on to major in illustration at the Fashion Institute of Technology in New York City. Nina now creates work for trade and educational publishing as well as kids' apps. Her work represents the beauty and diversity of our world. She currently lives in New Jersey with her husband, four-year-old daughter, and Tabi the cat.

Discover more
of the award-winning
What Does It Mean to Be…?® series